Anonymous

Suggestions to mothers

Anonymous

Suggestions to mothers

ISBN/EAN: 9783337763763

Printed in Europe, USA, Canada, Australia, Japan

Cover: Foto ©ninafisch / pixelio.de

More available books at **www.hansebooks.com**

By HANNAH McL. SHEPARD.

REVELATION OF SEX;

OR,

WHAT CHILDREN SHOULD KNOW,

By ELLEN H. SHELDON.

WASHINGTON :
PUBLISHED BY THE SOCIETY FOR MORAL EDUCATION.
1886.

SUGGESTIONS TO MOTHERS.

Enlightened motherhood, with its endowment of responsibility and conscientious endeavor faithfully to fulfil it to the uttermost, has no easy task to perform, however holy may be the effort or how beautiful and precious its fruits.

Nearly nineteen centuries have passed since the Immaculate Son was born, and only now are we beginning to learn the truths taught in the story of the maternity of Mary. We are just on the threshold of a proper appreciation of the higher responsibilities of motherhood, and only beginning to understand that they commence long before the birth of the child.

When the unborn babe lies, the tiniest germ in the matrix, its education has already begun. The observation of physiologists has determined the fact that even in the generative act the whole future of the offspring may be determined for weal or woe. The mother's thoughts while carrying her child beneath her bosom, her desires, her aspirations, her tempers, good or bad, her surroundings, physical and moral, all have an influence on the character that in the darkness and secrecy of her womb is being wrought out of all that she is.

The foregoing has a strong bearing on the special motive of this short treatise. The child whose pre-natal influences and conditions have been pure and wholesome; who comes into the world with a good organization, and who is carefully kept from contaminating companionship in its infancy and early years, will not be likely to develop untoward curiosity regarding sex or genesis. Sex will be dormant until the years arrive when it naturally and healthfully asserts itself and replies to its own inquiries. Nevertheless innocent or precocious inquisitiveness may be aroused, and when it is, it should not be trifled with. When the time arrives that the child desires to know concerning the origin of being, and is no longer satisfied with the simple answer, "God," to the question, "Who made you?" he should be answered seriously and in such a religious spirit that only a sacred impression will be made.

An excellent woman, who has brought up one of the loveliest families I ever knew, once said to me: "I never allowed myself to show any thought of sex toward my little ones. Boys and girls, when very small, were washed and dressed together, and I carefully avoided any observation that would contain in it any insinuation of shame being connected with one part of the body more than another; and when once looking at a picture, one of my children asked: "Mother, why do the Africans go naked?" I said, "Because they are ignorant and uncivilized. Civilized and Christian people wear clothes; they do not consider it proper to go about before each other naked." One of my boys said to me one day, when he and his twin-sister were being bathed, "Mother,

Kitty isn't made like me." I answered, "No; God makes all boys different from all girls." "Yes, I know," he said, "that's so their mothers will know them from each other and which to put trousers on." The child was satisfied, and so was I. I never had a minute's anxiety about my children's thoughts. After they grew to an age when it was desirable that the boys and girls should have separate rooms the change was made on the grounds of convenience. My sons and daughters, as long as they were at home, thought no harm of going in and out of each other's rooms as they pleased. They were accustomed, of course, to knock, but my daughters would not decline admission to their brothers because they were in the process of dressing. My sons who are married make good husbands. They are all pure, clean-living men, and have the highest regard for womanhood."

She said: "Do not misunderstand me; my children were not immodest; they were in many things individually more reserved than most children, but these reserves were on account of personality and not sex. One of my little boys would no sooner, after he was five or six years old, have run around naked before his brothers than before his sisters; and yet they, none of them, thought anything out of the way in seeing their sisters in their night dresses, or in helping them in their dressing, as buttoning underwaists, &c., and had any occasion of illness demanded it there was no service my boys would not readily have rendered to their sisters, or *vice versa*."

A child, the son of a dear friend, who had heard from another some prurient surmises as to the origin of babies, went to his mother and said : " Mamma, where *did* I come from ?   Johnnie —— says I come out of you ; did I, mamma?"   Said the mother, speaking of this to the writer, " I was astounded, and for a moment my heart stood still.   Here was a crisis I had never anticipated.   I had often thought that when my boy grew older—old enough—and was likely to have inquiry raised in his mind regarding such matters, that I would give him some good work on sexual physiology to read, and would talk seriously with him on matters of personal purity, but I had thought that the time was yet far away when my baby would require that I should reveal the mystery to him.   Now, the time had come prematurely ; all my plans were 'aglee,' and what was I to do?   I looked down at the flushed, eager, little face, and at once my mind was resolved.   I had never lied or prevaricated to my boy, and I would not now. 'Alfy,' I said, 'sit up on mother's lap, and I will tell you all that I can about it.'   I took the little fellow up and held his curly head against my breast where he could feel and hear the beating of my heart, and looking down into his clear, questioning eyes, I asked: 'Alfy, dear, who made you?' 'God,' he answered softly. 'Yes,' I said, 'God did make you.   His ways of making His creatures are very strange and beautiful and wonderful.   They are so wonderful that none of us can know all about it, and you are too young to understand as much as mother does, but she will tell you as much as she can.   When you were made, my dear, your father and I wanted a little child very much, and we asked God for it ; and one day mother felt a flutter like a bird moving right under her heart, and then she knew that it was the dear baby that God was making for her And, oh, Alfy, how mother prayed for the little life that she felt growing under her bosom every day, that it might be a dear, good child, and a blessing to father and mother and to all the world. And mother sewed little clothes for the baby that was coming, and into every seam she sewed hopes and prayers ; and by-and-by, after the little shirts and slips were all ready, the baby, my dear little Alfy, my precious little son, came into mother's arms. My dear, I cannot tell you all about that time—you couldn't understand now, and I know you will not ask. Mother was very ill and suffered great pain, such pain that she cried out with it; but when her baby, her darling child, was put into her arms she forgot the pain and tears and was glad, and thanked the good Lord for making her boy.' I pressed the dear child to my heart, and the little fellow raised up and with his eyes brimming over with tears, asked: 'Mamma, do mothers always suffer for their little children when God makes them ?' 'Yes, dear,' I answered, ' I think always ; but when children are good, and are so thoughtful, such comforts as my boy, they are not sorry, they are glad to have suffered for them.' 'Oh, mamma,' cried he, throwing his arms about my neck, 'how good children ought to be to mothers. I will be so good to you, mamma.'

"And he has been. From that day to this, and now

he is of age, there has been the most confiding companionship between us, and his tenderness and reverence toward me have been never failing.

"A day or two after I had answered his question, I said to him, 'Alfy, you remember what mother told you about your coming to her?' 'Yes, mamma.' 'Well, dear, I would rather you did not talk of those things to any one; will you promise?' 'Yes, mamma, dear,' he said; 'but why?' 'Because children do not rightly understand, and it is better they should not talk of what they don't know enough to talk intelligently.' From that time on he always came to me with his perplexities. His father was gone from us, and I had to be father and mother, too."

Keep your children as much as possible under your own eyes. Keep them from conversation or association with ignorant or unprincipled servants. For that matter have no person in your house in any capacity with whom you cannot trust your children. Allow no playmates who are not carefully and innocently trained. Teach your children from the time they are weaned to regard their parents as their best, most loving, most sympathizing friends, so that they will be sure to come to *you first* in any perplexity, any doubt, any trouble, or with any inquiry. Never fail them when they do so come. Be guided by circumstances as to how you frame your answer when they ask you, "How and whence came I?" but as you value their love and their wellbeing, let the answer contain nothing but the *truth*.

As soon as your children are old enough take them

yourself—not even their father can do this as well as
the mother who bore them—to some place where they
may see depicted the anatomy of the woman, and rev-
erentially explain to them the function of the womb.
I remember hearing or reading the following story, which
illustrates my meaning:

"One morning a young mother leading her seven-
year-old twins by the hand, entered the lecture-room of
Dr. S—— in Paris, just as he had dismissed his class,
and politely asked that herself and children might be
shown the large anatomical plates of the human body.
As one after another was exhibited and explained, the
plate showing the womb in the seventh month of preg-
nancy with twins, came in order; and as the doctor was
hastily withdrawing this without comment, the mother
said: 'Please do not lay that aside; it is the one of all
others I am most anxious that my children should see.
Be so kind as to explain it fully to them.' And placing
her little sons directly in front of it, said, 'You know,
my darlings, that I have told you that some day I would
show you a picture of the little room in my body where
you lived and slept so long a time before papa or I saw
you. We can't help loving one another as we do, when
you see how close to mother's heart you both lay for
nine happy months. By that time you had grown too
large to be comfortable in that warm room, and then it
opened for you to pass out into my arms. Dear little
sister lived there, and came to us in the same way; and
God lets all little babes have such homes in their mothers'
body until they are old enough to leave it. How sad it

would be if those who for so long a time lived so closely together should ever be unkind to one another.' Dr. S—— was moved to tears by this beautiful incident, and said to her, ' Madam, you have given to me, as well as to your children, the best explanation of that plate that was ever made. I cannot add a word.' And as she left the room, 'Ah!' said he, ' we need have no doubt as to the kind of men those sons will make, privileged as they are with such a mother and her pure instruction.'

" The knowledge that one mother had so thoroughly understood and performed her duty to innocent childhood, stimulated me to tell my sons, at an early age, the simple truth in a similar manner. And now, in their early manhood, the uprightness of their character, and the purity of their lives, their daily devotion to me and all womankind, is a glowing testimonial in favor of intelligent truth against falsehood and deception."

" Nature," says Grindon, " is a system of nuptials." That which is so universal, constantly taking place in every form of life, should not be made a mystery and uncanny secret of, to be pried into by false and sly methods. The minds of children may early be accustomed to the knowledge of the functions of sex with perfect innocence, and, indeed, by means of proper instruction, fortified and defended against prurient suggestion or morbid curiosity. There is no better way of accomplishing this than by lessons in botany. All children love flowers, and are easily interested in whatever pertains to them. Explain to them that blossoms are male and female; that they are fathers and mothers, and that the seed or fruit of the plant is the child of a father and mother after living in the blossom. Then take a lily, or some other simple flower, remove its petals, show to the children the stamens and pistils, and tell them that these are what enables the flower to have seed or fruit. The stamens are the males or fathers; the pistils are the females or the mothers. Show them the pollen, the delicate powder that hangs on the stamens. Open a pistil and show them the undeveloped seed germs; and explain to them how, when the pollen falls from the stamen to the sponge-like end of the pistil, it is taken in and causes the little germs to fructify and become seed. The magnifying glass or microscope will be a great help in these lessons. When they understand this, show them plants where the reproductive organs are in separate flowers, and instruct them that this is the case not only in the higher order of *plants*, but in all the higher order of life as in animals. In this way the knowledge of sex, its conditions and uses, will come so normally that there will be no possibility of any solacious thought connected with it or resulting from it.

WHAT CHILDREN SHOULD KNOW.

Many children of immature years are curious to know something of the vital processes of creation with which they are constantly surrounded. The advent of a baby brother or sister, or possibly the puzzling problem of their own origin and growth vexes their young minds, and they frequently propound questions, which in times past, have been answered falsely, evasively, or the little questioner unmercifully ridiculed and shamed for its importunity, and through this ignorance or carelessness the parent often loses the best and only opportunity of becoming the truest friend, confidant and adviser of the child.

The average intelligent child has been said to be a mere "interrogation point." It is of the utmost importance that the first impressions should be true and pure. It must necessarily learn its relation to all material objects through personal experience, or that knowledge must be imparted by wiser minds. A parent who would carelessly allow a child to grow up entirely ignorant of the effect of personal contact with fire or frost would be considered highly deserving of censure.

It is tacitly understood that the parent is to direct and guide the child in all the ordinary actions of life;

teaching that water will drown, fire burn, and frost chill. The mental and moral impressions which the young mind receives should be considered of equal importance with those relating to the physical world.

Combe, in his "Constitution of Man," speaking of "the evils that befall mankind from infringement of the organic laws," says: "It is a very common error to imagine that the feelings of the mind are communicated through the medium of the intellect; and, in particular, that if no indelicate objects reach the eyes, or expressions penetrate the ears, perfect purity will necessarily reign within the soul; but this principle of reasoning is fallacious and the result has been highly detrimental to society. The *feelings* have existence and acoivity distinct from the *intellect;* they spur it on to thtain their own gratification, and it may become either tbeir guide or their slave, according as it is or isnot enlightened concerning their constitution and oojects and the laws of nature to which they are subjected."

And speaking of the organ of amativeness, the largest of the whole mental organs, he says: "The whole question, therefore, resolves itself into this: whether it is more beneficial to cultivate the understanding, so as to dispose and enable it to control and direct that faculty, or under the influence of an error in philosophy and false delicacy founded on it, to permit it to riot in all the fierceness of a blind, animal instinct, withdrawn from the eye of reason, but not thereby deprived of its vehemence and importunity."

This is authoritative testimony in favor of a cultivated intellect as a guide and controlling power of the amative instinct, an instinct which embraces all the best qualities of humanity, all love, tenderness and sympathy; the social qualities, the most admirable which human beings possess, but whose blind, reckless expression through merely physical attraction degrades and sensualizes life to a purely animal standard.

The precocity of many children is daily recognized. Michelet, the great French writer, describing the brain of a child, calls it a " hieroglyphic flower." He says: " The brain of a child, seen from its base, has all the effect of a large and splendid camellia, with its ivory nerves, its delicate, rosy veins, and its pale, azure tint. It is of an immaculate whiteness, and yet of an exquisite and tender softness of which nothing else can give an idea, and which, to my mind, leaves every other earthly thing far behind." In examining the brains of children, he frequently found the convolutions and folds more neatly arranged, more finely traced than in those of many common women of twenty-five or even thirty-five years.

He says: " The nerves of motion are developed and active before the counterpoising forces which maintain the equilibrium. Thus its incessant restlessness annoys and often vexes us. We do not reflect that at this age the child is life itself."

" The nerves of sensation are mature, consequently the child's capacity to suffer and even to love. An astonishing fact in connection with this tender age is, that amorous sensibility is expressed in the nerves more strongly than in the adult."

" I was alarmed at this; love, slumbering as yet in the sexual organs, seemed already fully awakened in those parts of the spinal marrow which act on those organs."

The early awakening of the amative nature through nervous sensibility in the brain and spinal marrow before the maturing of the procreative power, the capacity of love and tenderness which even the immature possess, show us plainly the necessity of the control of those functions by the brain, and of being early and intelligently instructed as to their uses, and that we have our choice of its intelligent guidance, or, as Combe so forcibly expresses it, " permit it to riot in all the fierceness of a blind animal instinct, withdrawn from the eye of reason but not thereby deprived of its vehemence and importunity."

A *true* mother will have prepared her child's mind for the reception of the truth in relation to the natural development of physical life; leading along from the germinative processes of the vegetable and floral kingdom to that of the animal, showing the gradual and natural gradation from inorganic to organic life, and the different requirements of each.

Michelet says, in *La Femme*, " nothing is easier than the revelation of sex to a child.thus prepared. For her who is kept in ignorance of its general laws, who learns the whole mystery at once it is a serious and a dangerous thing. What are we to think of the imprudence of those parents who leave this revelation to chance? For what is chance? It is often some companion neither

innocent nor pure of imagination; oftener than would
be believed it is a flippant, sensual speech from some
near relative However that may be, if this mystery
be not revealed by the mother it may be overwhelming
and blasting, annihilating the judgment. At such a
time, before she recovers herself, the poor little one is,
as it were, at one's mercy. As for her who has early
and naturally learned of the generation of plants and
of insects, who knows that in every species life renews
itself from the egg, and that all nature is engaged in the
perpetual labor of ovolation, she is not at all astonished
to find herself subject to the same common law. The
peculiar changes which every month accompany the
phenomenon seem also very natural when she has seen
the same laborious processes in the inferior creatures.
All this appears to be noble, grand, and pure, as it har-
monizes with the general law of creation. Grander still
when she sees in it the continual restoration of what
death destroys."

WHERE DO BABIES COME FROM?

Happy the mother who, intelligently foreseeing the
inevitable moment when this or a similar question will
be propounded to her, can gather the loved questioner
to her heart and say:

My dear, papa and mamma loved each other so dearly
that we felt we would always like to live together in the
same house, to love and care for each other, enjoy our
youth together, and grow old in each other's company.

After a time we thought we would be glad to have a

little child in our home; one which was our very own, and so we chose you for our little one to live with us and be loved by us. And now you wish to know "where you came from?" Everything grows as you have seen. Everything passes through a process which is called growth or development, from what is called a germ, which is sometimes a seed, sometimes an egg. The seeds from which all trees and plants and flowers come are placed in the earth, where, lying in the darkness for a time, warmed by the sun's rays, and moistened by the rain, the outer part of the seed breaks open and a portion of it forces its way upward into the light and air, while other parts of it grow down into the ground to gain food from the earth. Plants and vegetables are not able to move about to obtain the food they need, so remain in the earth and receive nourishment from it. All animal life comes from an egg, or ovum, as it is sometimes called. You have seen the egg of the hen, in which the chickens grow. The mother hen sits upon the eggs, and the warmth of her body helps them to grow and when the chickens have grown large enough and are all covered with pretty down, they pick their way out of the shell into the light and air, where they can grow into big hens.

Where do babies grow? In a place prepared for them in the mother's body. Mamma and you lived together all the time you were growing into a little baby, and got strong enough to live in mamma's arms, lie in her bosom, and bear the light and air of this world.

How long does it take for babies to grow from the

egg? For nine long months, almost a year, you lived in the little room in mamma's body, in the "house not made with hands," which the Creator has so nicely prepared for the protection and development of her children. Here, folded closely like the petals of a rosebud, you grew into that most wonderful thing which can ever be created—a little baby.

Where does the egg come from? The eggs grow in the mother's body, and the food she eats is taken up by the blood vessels and used to form the bones and flesh of her baby's body

How did you get your food while living in mamma's body? A portion of the food mamma ate was prepared and sent through the blood vessels in her body to feed and nourish you.

Do trees and plants and animals have papas and mammas? Yes. They are called the male and female trees and plants and animals; and they both help to make the seeds or eggs grow. The female or mother plants are the kinds which bear the blossoms and flowers and fruit. The apples and pears, and all fruits and flowers, are the children of the trees, plants, and vines. Sometimes the male and female plants live on the same bush, and when they do not they must be placed near each other, so as to help each other in the growth of their fruit or flower children. When you are older you can better understand all these processes.

The body which your papa and mamma gave you is the home which you are to continue to build and in which you must live when you grow up. When you lived in mamma's body with her she was very careful to eat proper food so as to give you the best material she could to begin building this house, and now you must learn to put the best material you can into this wonderful building, that you may enjoy living in it when you grow up to be a man or woman. Your eyes are the windows of the house, having fringed curtains to shut out the light when you desire to do so. If you wish to have a clear, bright outlook and pleasant views you must keep the whole house in good order, as you cannot injure any part of it without affecting the whole.

Some day when you grow up and find a friend whom you can love and wish to live with as papa and mamma do, you too may desire to become father or mother to a little child, and only by keeping your body clean and pure can you have healthy and happy children.

The living room of this building is the upper story, the head, where you can enjoy the pleasant sights and sounds and tastes and smells. Here is where you live and direct the care of the other portions of the dwelling. Your hands and feet are your servants, and if you take care of them and guide them well they will always do your bidding willingly.

If you have good and pure thoughts and hang up pleasant pictures on the walls of your memory in this upper story you will have a beautiful home to live in when you are old. You cannot move out of it if you do not like it when you have built it unless you are willing to stay out. You can never return to it if you leave it. If you injure this house by making yourself sick you will have an uncomfortable prison to live in instead of a beautiful home.